C000243806

Paul Shannon
Blue Diesel Days

Ian Allan
PUBLISHING

Dedication
To Babette

Acknowledgements
I am grateful to Hugh Ballantyne, David Cross, John Edgington, John Feild, Stewart Jolly, Michael Mensing, Gavin Morrison, Geoff Plumb and Michael Rhodes for their willingness to loan historic material for this book and for providing useful information for the captions. I also wish to thank David Rapson for his generous help over a period of many years.

Bibliography
S. K. Baker: *Rail Atlas of Great Britain and Ireland*, various editions (Oxford Publishing Co)

Geoffrey Body: *Britain's Rail Routes Past and Present: The East Coast Main Line* (Silver Link Publishing, 1995)

David N. Clough and D. I. Rapson: *Locomotive Recognition: Class 37s* (Ian Allan Publishing, 1991)

Tom Noble: *Diesels on the Regions: Scotland* (Oxford Publishing Co, 1984)

Brian Reed: *Diesel-hydraulic Locomotives of the Western Region* (David & Charles, 1974)

Michael Rhodes: *British Marshalling Yards* (Oxford Publishing Co, 1988)

Michael Rhodes and Paul Shannon: *Freight Only* volumes 1, 2 and 3 (Silver Link Publishing, 1987/8)

British Railways Locomotives and Other Motive Power, combined volume, various editions (Ian Allan Publishing)

British Railways Pre-Grouping Atlas and Gazetteer (Ian Allan Publishing, 1972)

Locomotive Stock Book (Railway Correspondence & Travel Society, 1966 and 1969)

Locoshed Book, various editions (Ian Allan Publishing)

Various issues of *Modern Railways*, *Rail Enthusiast*, *The Railway Magazine*, the *Railway Observer* and *Railway World*

Front cover:
'Deltic' No 55 011 The Royal Northumberland Fusiliers emerges from Welwyn South Tunnel with the 09.36 Hull–King's Cross on 25 September 1981. *Paul Shannon*

Back cover:
Class 33/0 No 33 031 arrives at Westbury on 29 July 1982 with the 12.14 from Bristol Temple Meads to Portsmouth Harbour. The lower-quadrant semaphores would soon be swept away, but the locomotive was to remain in traffic until 1989. *Michael Mensing*

Title page:
No 40 057 emerges from Rise Hill Tunnel, near Dent, with an up freight working on 2 July 1976. *Michael Mensing*

First published 2007

ISBN (10) 0 7110 3225 4
ISBN (13) 978 0 7110 3225 5

Published by Ian Allan Publishing
an imprint of Ian Allan Publishing Ltd, Hersham, Surrey
KT12 4RG

Printed in England by Ian Allan Printing Ltd, Hersham, Surrey KT12 4RG

Code: 0711/C1

Visit the Ian Allan Publishing website at
www.ianallanpublishing.com

Contents

Introduction 5

Scottish Region 6

Eastern Region 22

London Midland Region 44

Southern Region 72

Western Region 78

The sheer variety of BR diesel-locomotive classes in the 1970s was often taken for granted, especially by those still mourning the end of steam. With examples of Classes 40, 25 and 45 visible in the background, No 31 326 leaves the then recently remodelled Peterborough station with a down mixed freight on 3 July 1974. *Hugh Ballantyne*

Swindon-built Class 42 'Warship' No 807 *Caradoc* heads east at Teignmouth with a mixed freight on 30 August 1972. The load includes empty Motorail flats as well as short-wheelbase opens that were probably used on china-clay traffic. Less than a month later *Caradoc* was withdrawn. *Gavin Morrison*

Introduction

In 1965 the face of British Railways underwent its most radical change since Nationalisation, as regional colour schemes gave way to a corporate identity, with Rail blue as the dominant colour. An exhibition held at the Design Centre in London featured the launch of a design manual for rail staff which specified not only the new liveries of blue for locomotives and suburban rolling-stock and blue-and-grey for main-line rolling-stock, similar to those that had been trialled on 'XP64' stock in the previous year, but also a new style of black-on-white lettering for station signs and printed material. British Railways became British Rail, and, most enduringly of all, the double-arrow logo was adopted as the national railway symbol.

The timing of the livery change, just as the last first-generation diesels were rolling off the production line, meant that BR faced a huge repainting programme. Only a small number of locomotives carried blue livery from new, including the Class 50s, most Class 73s and a few Class 25s and 47s. The process of repainting took some years to complete: in early 1975 green livery was still carried by nearly 300 shunters and 200 main-line locomotives. No exceptions were allowed, and even the narrow-gauge steam locomotives of BR's Vale of Rheidol Railway assumed the corporate identity. Minor variations took place in the positioning of numbers and logos on diesel locomotives, but essentially the colours and designs launched in 1965 remained unchanged until the 1980s.

While Rail blue was often dismissed as boring by those who remembered the individuality of the regions, in turn recalling the days of the pre-1948 'Big Four', railway operations in the 1970s were a fascinating mixture of old and new. Much of the infrastructure of the steam age was still in place, express trains were virtually all locomotive-hauled, and loose-coupled pick-up goods trains still ambled along rural branch lines on some parts of the network. The traction fleet was diverse, with several types that were restricted to certain regions. However, rapid change was taking place. Back in 1967 BR had decreed that its main-line diesel fleet should reduce by 1974 from 2,976 of 28 types to 2,240 of just 15 types. The least reliable and least numerous classes were naturally the first to go, but the later casualties would include the entire fleet of diesel-hydraulics supplied to the Western Region.

The introduction of High Speed Train (later InterCity 125) units on the Western Region in 1976 and on the East Coast main line in 1978 marked the first definite move away from traditional locomotive haulage. However, BR continued to use its sizeable fleet of locomotives, increasingly fitted with electric train heating (ETH), on cross-country services and on certain routes from London, such as Waterloo–Exeter and Liverpool Street–Norwich. Locomotive haulage even took over from DMUs on several lines, such as Crewe–Cardiff and Edinburgh–Glasgow. Further secondary routes would see a temporary return to hauled stock in the 1980s. On the freight side, the change in traction policy was less dramatic but included the introduction of BR's Class 56 locomotives, the first 83 examples being outshopped in the 1965 Rail-blue style.

Perhaps the first sign of Rail blue's eventual demise was the painting in 1979 of white window surrounds on Finsbury Park's 'Deltics'. The large-logo livery style appeared in the following year, and the 1980s would see a proliferation of liveries as BR reorganised itself into business sectors. But Rail blue did not disappear overnight: many Class 20 and Class 31 locomotives retained blue livery in the early 1990s, and a good number of Class 08 shunters kept the colour scheme going into the 21st century.

Today Rail blue has earned its place as one of the heritage liveries displayed on preserved lines. Arguably many locomotives looked better in earlier — or later — colour schemes, but the sight of Rail blue conjures up memories of a very different railway system from the one that we have today.

ONE

Scottish Region

Diesels were well established in Scotland by the time BR blue livery first appeared. Steam had been eliminated from the Highlands in the early 1960s and was gone from the rest of Scotland by the end of 1966. Many passenger services were operated by diesel multiple-units, not only on suburban routes but also on some InterCity lines such as Inverness–Aberdeen, Glasgow–Ayr and Glasgow–Edinburgh. But there was also plenty of work for locomotives, ranging from expresses on the East and West Coast main lines to freight duties throughout the country.

The vagaries of the 1955 Modernisation Plan had left Scotland with a wide variety of locomotive classes. Main-line types allocated to Scottish depots in 1969 comprised Classes 17, 20, 24, 25, 26, 27, 29, 37, 40, 47 and 55, while the Crewe-based Class 50s worked regularly to Glasgow. The dominance of low-powered types is striking, and this led to frequent double-heading on routes such as the Highland main line to Inverness. The use of Class 47s north of the border at that time was limited to a few duties on the East Coast main line.

The Scottish diesel-shunter fleet in 1969 comprised just two types: Classes 06 and 08. While Class 08 needs little introduction, Class 06 was a uniquely Scottish design, its high power rating and short wheelbase making it well suited to heavily trafficked dockside lines. Withdrawals started in the 1960s, but two examples lingered until 1981. One Class 06 has since been preserved.

As on BR as a whole, the less successful diesel types were quickly eliminated. Only a few of the ill-fated North British Class 29s — re-engined variants of the notoriously unreliable Class 21s — remained in use long enough to receive blue livery. The last Class 29s succumbed in 1971, and none survived into preservation: the memory of steam was too recent for enthusiasts at that time to invest time and money in saving a diesel.

The centre-cab Clayton Class 17s were used in North East England and Cumbria as well as Scotland, but they mainly associated with Scotland, and that is where the last survivors ended up, working freight trains in the Central Belt and Ayrshire. Of an original fleet of 117 locomotives, 33 were withdrawn in 1968, 12 in 1969 and the remaining 72 by the end of 1971. One example survived in industrial use and was subsequently preserved.

The Birmingham Railway Carriage & Wagon Co Classes 26 and 27 were as distinctively Scottish as Classes 29 and 17, but far more successful. The Class 26s provided staple power for services out of Inverness as well as working from Haymarket; the fleet remained largely intact into the early 1980s, and the last example was not withdrawn until 1993. The Class 27s did not last quite as long, but among their duties in the 1970s was the Glasgow–Edinburgh high-speed push-pull operation, for which 24 examples were specially modified. The changed emphasis of preservation since the 1970s is illustrated by the fact that no fewer than 13 Class 26s and eight Class 27s survive today in private ownership.

A few Class 37s had been based in Scotland since 1968, but it was not until 1981 that the type became established on passenger and freight trains on the West Highland line, followed a year later by their takeover of services to Kyle of Lochalsh, Thurso and Wick. Their freight duties included double-headed iron-ore trains from Hunterston to Ravenscraig. Class 47s also became more prominent in Scotland following the withdrawal of other classes.

By the late 1980s BR blue was giving way to the bright new colours of the BR business sectors, and locomotive haulage on passenger trains was giving way to second-generation diesel units. Traditional patterns of locomotive allocation ceased to be relevant: Haymarket depot lost its entire main-line locomotive fleet, concentrating instead on maintaining diesel units, and even Eastfield, which in 1988 still had more than 120 locomotives on its books, faced closure in 1994 in favour of a dedicated but much smaller freight depot at Motherwell.

Above:
Class 20 locomotives usually worked in pairs but could turn up singly on shunting and light freight duties. A long-standing Scottish member of the class, No 20 119, approaches Ardrossan Harbour with empty bitumen tanks for loading on 18 July 1984. This locomotive was withdrawn from Toton depot in 1992 but was saved from the cutter's torch and is based at Barrow Hill engine shed at the time of writing. *Paul Shannon*

Below:
Withdrawal of the Class 27 fleet was already underway when No 27 014 was photographed pausing for a token exchange at Glenwhilly at the head of train 1S40, the 05.13 Euston–Stranraer Harbour parcels, on 25 July 1985. Although the platforms were still *in situ* Glenwhilly had closed to passengers in 1965. *Paul Shannon*

Above:
Although the Class 50s were designed for the West Coast main line, they also appeared on the Glasgow & South Western route via Kilmarnock and Dumfries. No D419 passes Kilmarnock with a 1Z60 test train from Glasgow to Carlisle in 1970. This locomotive became No 50 019 under the TOPS scheme and was named *Ramillies* after its transfer to the Western Region; it has since been preserved on the Mid Norfolk Railway. *David Cross*

Below:
At Falkland Yard on 12 July 1988, No 37 066 waits while ground staff carry out final checks on the first wagon of train 6S59, the 01.35 from Tees Yard to Falkland, specially extended on this occasion to Stranraer. The train is conveying steel from Lackenby and Scunthorpe and cars from Immingham, Cowley and Longbridge, all destined for export from Stranraer to Northern Ireland. *Paul Shannon*

Above:
In a bold — for the time — departure from the BR corporate image, a number of Mk 1 coaches were decorated in Sealink livery to work boat trains between Glasgow and Stranraer. No 47 145 passes Dalry with the 11.30 departure from Glasgow Central on 18 July 1984. *Paul Shannon*

Below:
The centre-cab 'Claytons', designated Class 17, were one of the biggest failures of 'dieselisation'. A catalogue of major defects forced them to spend long periods out of service and soon BR decided that the best option was withdrawal. The class became extinct on BR in 1971, less than 10 years after its introduction. No D8606 shunts coal wagons at Hawick on 5 January 1969. *Gavin Morrison*

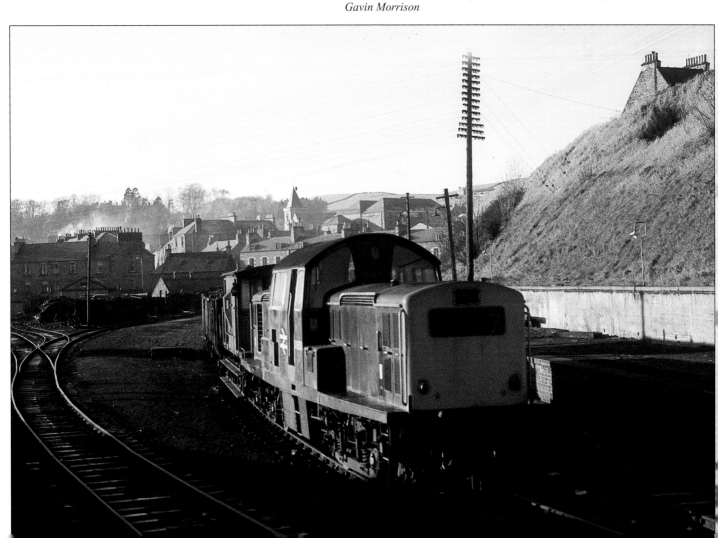

Sporting a Railway Correspondence & Travel Society headboard, Class 55 'Deltic' No D9007 *Pinza* pauses at Riccarton Junction with the 'Farewell to the Waverley Route' railtour on 5 January 1969, the last full day of operation for this once important Anglo-Scottish route. Today the northern section of the Waverley route between Edinburgh and Tweedbank is poised for reopening, but it seems unlikely that main-line trains will return to Riccarton Junction. *Gavin Morrison*

Two white elephants in one photograph: the vast expanse of Millerhill marshalling yard, opened in 1962/3 but destined never to fulfil its potential because of the sharp decline in wagonload traffic, forms the backdrop for this view of soon to be condemned Class 17 'Clayton' No D8529 on 7 September 1971. *David Cross*

Classes 24 and 26 had compatible control systems, which meant they could work in multiple. Nos 24 120 and 26 041 pass Haymarket West Junction with the 13.35 Edinburgh–Inverness train on 20 April 1976. Both locomotives have tablet-catching recesses visible on the nearest cabside, while the Class 24 has had its front gangway doors sealed to prevent draughts. *Gavin Morrison*

Haymarket was one of the two major diesel depots in Scotland in the 1970s, the other being Eastfield. Haymarket's allocation included Classes 08, 20, 24, 25, 26, 27, 40, 47 and 55. Pictured on shed at Haymarket on 19 April 1976 are Nos 40 158 and 24 118. *Gavin Morrison*

Above:
Two batches of Class 40s were delivered new to the Scottish Region, Nos D260–6 and D357–68. They were all allocated to Haymarket depot but worked on suitable routes throughout Scotland. No D262 stands at the head of a train of locally manufactured Austin cars at Bathgate on 7 September 1971. The D260–6 batch had been built without headcode panels but had had these fitted in the late 1960s — somewhat ironic, given that the Scottish Region made less use of headcodes than did other regions. *Derek Cross*

Below:
A total of 69 Birmingham RCW Co 1,250hp locomotives, later known as Class 27, was introduced in 1961/62. They spent most of their working life in Scotland, working a range of passenger and freight duties, and some were later fitted with push-pull equipment for the Glasgow–Edinburgh high-speed service. No 27 014 stands at St Rollox Works, Glasgow, on 25 April 1982. *John Feild*

Above:
The uniformity of the BR corporate image is emphasised in this view of Eastfield depot on 4 September 1977. ETH-fitted Class 47 No 47 464 is nearest the camera, while Classes 08, 37, 25, 27 and 20 are also represented. Eastfield's allocation numbered more than 200 locomotives at that time. *Gavin Morrison*

Below:
The exotic rubs shoulders with the ordinary: a visit to Eastfield depot open day on 17 September 1972 finds sparklingly pristine 'Deltic' No D9021 *Argyll & Sutherland Highlander* stabled alongside locally-based Class 27 No D5362. On the left is an even less familiar sight at this normally diesel-only location, Class 83 electric No 83 005. *Derek Cross*

Top:
**With the Forth Bridge towering above the skyline, No 47 524 enters Dalmeny station on 24 May 1975 with the 1E29 Aberdeen–
King's Cross express, comprising mainly early Mk 2 stock. Built in 1966 as No D1107, No 47 524 it was allocated to various Eastern
Region depots before transfer to the Scottish Region in 1988. It was retired from main-line service in 1997 but survives today on the
Churnet Valley Railway.** *Gavin Morrison*

Above:
**Metropolitan-Cammell units were among the more successful first-generation DMU designs, being allocated to the Scottish, Eastern
and London Midland regions. Here a trio of two-car Metropolitan-Cammell units takes the Cumbernauld line at Greenhill Lower
Junction with a diverted Dundee–Glasgow Queen Street service on 17 September 1972.** *Derek Cross*

Top:
In 1974 BR introduced a daytime passenger service between London and Inverness, named the 'Clansman'. The service continued running throughout the 1980s. No 47 610 hauls the 11-coach 10.20 Inverness–Euston under a fine gantry of semaphores at Stirling on 19 July 1984. The semaphores would still be there two decades later, while No 47 610 — later renumbered 47 823 and then 47 787 — retired from revenue-earning service with EWS in 2004 but at the time of writing looks likely to make a return with West Coast Railways. *Paul Shannon*

Above:
No 26 021 stands in Perth station with the 08.30 Inverness–Edinburgh service on 22 June 1982. At that time all regular passenger services via Perth were locomotive-hauled, and there was substantial parcels and mail traffic too — as shown by the two rakes of vans on the left. No 26 021 was withdrawn in 1991 and scrapped by MC Metals in Glasgow. *Paul Shannon*

Above:
The Class 27s were still active in the mid-1980s on passenger and freight duties. No 27 056 has just crossed the Tay Bridge as it heads south with the 15.28 from Dundee to Edinburgh on 21 July 1984. This locomotive had previously been used on Edinburgh–Glasgow push-pull duties as No 27 112; it later passed into preservation and at the time of writing is based on the Northampton & Lamport Railway. *Paul Shannon*

Below:
No 47 040 stands at Montrose station with the 09.20 departure from Aberdeen on 22 March 1981. The goods crane on the right was a notable relic from the days when almost every station had its own goods yard. The locomotive spent the first 15 years of its life based on the London Midland Region before moving north of the border in 1980. It later carried the numbers 47 642 and 47 766 and was withdrawn from front-line duties in 2000. *Paul Shannon*

Right:
The Scottish Region's diminutive Class 06 shunters were an early target for withdrawal. Only 10 members of the 35-strong class survived long enough to be renumbered into the TOPS series, and the last example was withdrawn in 1981. No 06 006 is pictured at Aberdeen Ferryhill depot on 26 June 1976.
Paul Shannon

Below:
Until the early 1980s Aberdeen boasted a fine selection of semaphore signals. No 40 065 pulls away from Aberdeen station on 2 September 1977 with empty grain hoppers from Burghead, a distinctive block-train working which served the Scottish whisky industry throughout the 1970s. *Gavin Morrison*

Above:
Short locomotive-hauled trains were a feature of several lines in the Highlands of Scotland. Here Class 27 No D5360 skirts Loch Eilt, west of Glenfinnan, with a service from Mallaig on 4 June 1971. The Mallaig extension line led a precarious existence in the 1970s, but its prospects improved once BR began to market its tourist potential more energetically, including regular steam-hauled workings in the summer. *Gavin Morrison*

Below:
No 37 112 approaches Corrour station with the first train of the day from Fort William on 28 August 1981. The Mk 1 coaches are still in BR corporate blue and grey but the locomotive sports wrap-around yellow ends, one of the first challenges to the standardisation policy of the 1960s. Class 37s had only recently taken over West Highland duties from Class 27s when this photograph was taken. *Paul Shannon*

Above:
**Nos 26 027 and 26 039 arrive at Invergordon with the 11.00
from Inverness to Wick and Thurso on 22 June 1981.
The scene retains many steam-age features, including the
Highland Railway goods shed, the 'door to door' container used
as a static store beside the shed, the telegraph poles and the blue
running-in board above the leading locomotive.** *Michael Rhodes*

Bottom:
**The Far North outpost of Georgemas Junction witnessed the
regular shunting of locomotive-hauled passenger trains in the
days when all services to and from Inverness conveyed portions
for both Thurso and Wick. No 26 021 prepares to depart from
Georgemas Junction with the Thurso portion of the afternoon
train from Inverness on 14 August 1981. Second-generation
diesel units took over Far North passenger workings in 1989.**
Paul Shannon

Showing the twin headlights, sealed front gangway and token-exchange recess that were distinctive features of the Scottish Class 24s, No D5121 is pictured at Achnasheen while working a Kyle train on 10 March 1973. *Gavin Morrison*

TWO

Eastern Region

Covering a diverse area from the Fenlands of East Anglia and busy commuter lines around London to the prestigious East Coast main line and the busy industrial networks of Yorkshire and the North East, the Eastern Region was host to a wide variety of locomotive types in the BR blue era. Main-line locomotives allocated to Eastern Region depots in 1969 comprised Classes 15, 17, 20, 23, 24, 25, 31, 37, 40, 45, 46, 47 and 55.

Early casualties were the British Thomson-Houston Class 15s, the Clayton Class 17s and the English Electric 'Baby Deltic' Class 23s, all of which were extinct by the end of 1971. The demise of these classes pre-dated any serious interest in diesel preservation, although one Class 15 and one Scottish Class 17 did manage to survive, in both cases thanks to a period in industrial or departmental use following withdrawal from the main line.

Although they worked on many parts of the BR network, Classes 31 and 37 were very familiar traction on Eastern Region lines throughout the blue period. In 1969 all but five of the Class 31s were allocated to Eastern Region depots, shared between Finsbury Park, Stratford, March, Immingham and Tinsley. Ten years later they still had an Eastern Region bias, some now being based in the North East at Thornaby and Gateshead. Towards the end of the BR blue period those Class 31s fitted with electric train heating took over temporarily from first-generation DMUs on cross-country services to and from East Anglia and South Humberside. The 19 members of the non-standard '31/0' sub-class had been withdrawn between 1976 and 1980, but many of the remaining Class 31s lasted into the 1990s, and a few are still working at the time of writing.

The Class 37 is arguably the most successful design of diesel locomotive supplied to BR. The first batch had cut its teeth on the Great Eastern main line back in 1961, and well over 100 were delivered new to Eastern Region depots. By 1969 examples were allocated to Stratford, March, Tinsley, Healey Mills, York, Thornaby and Gateshead. They worked a wide variety of freight services, while their passenger duties included Liverpool Street–King's Lynn expresses and the Harwich–Manchester boat train. They were also a popular choice for Summer Saturday holiday trains. By the late 1970s more than half of the fleet was still based on the Eastern Region, but the 1980s would see some transferred to other regions as replacements for withdrawn classes. Apart from one early accident victim, the class remained intact until 1987, and withdrawals did not gather pace until the 1990s. At the time of writing a number remain in use with Direct Rail Services, West Coast Railways and EWS.

Although more restricted in their operations than Classes 31 and 37, the Class 55 'Deltics' were the flagship locomotives of the East Coast main line for two decades and arguably earned greater fame than did any other BR diesel class. They will long be remembered for maintaining demanding schedules on the 'Hull Executive', then Britain's fastest train, and on the King's Cross–York 'semi-fasts', which actually consisted of a series of tightly-timed sprints between intermediate stations. The first 'Deltic' diagram went over to InterCity 125s in 1978, and BR's final 'Deltic'-hauled special ran in January 1981. But that was, of course, far from the end of the story. Six 'Deltics' have been preserved, all of which are registered with Network Rail, although only one is currently passed for main-line running.

At the other end of the spectrum, large numbers of Class 03 shunters worked from Eastern Region depots during the BR blue period, with particular concentrations in East Anglia and the North East. Their route availability of 1, compared with 5 for a Class 08, made them useful for working lightly laid sidings. The withdrawal of the Class 03s from BR stock spanned a long period, from 1968 to 1989, but many enjoyed a second lease of life in industrial use, and more than 50 examples survive in the hands of preservationists.

Above:
For more than 150 years Stratford was a major location for railway engineering and locomotive maintenance. Pictured on 4 December 1980 inside the engine-repair shop, which dated back to 1915, are 'Deltic' No 55 005 *The Prince of Wales's Own Regiment of Yorkshire* and No 31 255. Today the site of Stratford Works, depot and freight terminal is being redeveloped in connection with the Channel Tunnel Rail Link. *Paul Shannon*

Below:
The Wickham DMU design was not a success, and all five two-car units had been withdrawn from service by 1971. However, one unit was converted into a General Manager's saloon and continued to run on the main line until 1980. Here it makes a colourful sight as it passes Tottenham Hale on 6 June 1979. After a lengthy period out of use the unique unit has since been given a third lease of life thanks to a grant from the Heritage Lottery Fund; at the time of writing it is based on the Llangollen Railway. *Paul Shannon*

The Birmingham Railway Carriage & Wagon Co Class 104 units remained in Rail-blue livery for longer than most other DMU types. A two-car unit comprising cars 53479 and 53437 approaches Leytonstone High Road station with the 10.45 from Gospel Oak to Barking on 28 October 1987. *Paul Shannon*

On a route that is closed at the time of writing for conversion to a new branch of the Docklands Light Railway, No 37 087 passes Stratford Market with a lightly loaded trip working from Temple Mills Yard to Silvertown on 4 July 1989. The wagons would be loaded with scrap metal for Aldwarke, conveyed at that time by the Speedlink wagonload network. *Paul Shannon*

Above:
'Deltics' were not commonplace at Cambridge but appeared from time to time on diversions when the East Coast main line was blocked by weekend engineering works. No 55 017 *The Durham Light Infantry* pulls away from Cambridge with the 20.05 Aberdeen–King's Cross sleeper on 27 April 1980. *Paul Shannon*

Below:
Before electrification, services between London and King's Lynn were invariably locomotive-hauled, Classes 31 and 37 giving way to Class 47 traction in later years. With the semaphore signal and telegraph poles creating a nostalgic feel, No 47 115 passes Waterbeach with a London-bound train on 20 April 1981. *Paul Shannon*

Above:
The small yard at Cambridge remained a hive of freight activity until the early 1980s, with traffic from local terminals adding to the through traffic on wagonload trains between Temple Mills and Whitemoor. On 13 November 1979 No 37 047 departs Cambridge with train 8J88 from Temple Mills, comprising a fascinating mixture of air-braked, vacuum-braked and unfitted wagons. Resignalling would soon transform this scene forever. *Paul Shannon*

Below:
One of the original fleet of ETH-fitted Class 31s, No 31 410, crosses the flooded Hundred Foot Washes, between Manea and Ely, with the 12.50 Peterborough–Harwich Parkeston Quay train on 16 February 1985. Locomotive-hauled trains provided a stopgap on this route between first- and second-generation DMUs. *Paul Shannon*

Above:
A Cravens Class 105 unit, comprising cars E56435 and E51262, enters Wrabness station with the 11.40 Manningtree–Harwich Town local on 8 April 1983. The route has since been electrified and resignalled, while Wrabness station has become an unstaffed halt. *Paul Shannon*

Below:
Several East Anglian depots had allocations of Class 03 shunters in the 1970s, but Norwich was unique in the Region in having only '03s' and no '08s'. With the passenger terminus and cathedral in the background, No 03 020 shunts air-braked vans and vacuum-braked open wagons on 18 September 1975. *Hugh Ballantyne*

Above:
In a delightful railway setting showing little change since steam days, No 31 217 approaches Reedham station with the 14.12 Saturdays-only train from Yarmouth to Manchester Piccadilly on 9 June 1984. The Class 31 worked the train as far as Norwich, where a Class 47 would take over. *Stewart Jolly*

Below:
'Deltic' No 55 001 *St Paddy* produces a neat plume of exhaust as it moves on to King's Cross stabling point on the morning of 10 July 1976. No 55 001 was withdrawn before 'Deltic' mania reached its peak and was therefore one of the least-photographed members of the class. *Gavin Morrison*

Top:
In 1992 more than half of the Class 08 shunter fleet was still in BR blue livery. On 17 February No 08 709 shunts bogie hopper wagons at King's Cross Freight Terminal. The wagons had carried sea-dredged aggregates from Angerstein Wharf on the south bank of the Thames Estuary. Today the site of King's Cross Freight Terminal has been swallowed up by the Channel Tunnel Rail Link, while replacement freight facilities have been provided just outside St Pancras. *Paul Shannon*

Above:
An unidentified Class 31, running light-engine under headcode 0B03, approaches the road bridge on the north side of Wood Green station, adjacent to Wood Green Up 'box No 2, in October 1970. A fellow Class 31 is in the carriage sidings alongside Bounds Green depot, while a Class 47 can be glimpsed heading away onto the Hertford loop. *Geoff Plumb*

Above:
A small variation on BR blue was the painting of white cab-window surrounds on Finsbury Park 'Deltics'. No 55 015 *Tulyar* races through Welwyn North station with the 12.34 Hull–King's Cross service on 17 April 1981. After withdrawal *Tulyar* was acquired by the Deltic Preservation Society and at the time of writing resides at Barrow Hill. *Paul Shannon*

Below:
In the early 1980s the Barrow Hill area was a fascinating freight backwater, with numerous Class 20-hauled trip workings to and from local collieries and plenty of mechanical signalling still in use. Nos 20 023 and 20 001 depart from Seymour sidings, on the Bolsover branch, with a trainload of MDV coal wagons on 27 July 1981. No 20 001 survives in the ownership of the Class 20 Locomotive Society. *Paul Shannon*

Right

Three Class 13 'master and slave' units were created in 1965 by coupling two Class 08s together and removing one of the cabs. They were used exclusively at Tinsley marshalling yard and remained in service until the mid-1980s. No 13 003, formerly numbered D4500 and converted from Nos D3698 and D4188, pushes its train from the reception sidings towards the hump at Tinsley on 29 July 1976. *Gavin Morrison*

Below:

Because of their single cabs and low power rating the Class 20s usually operated in pairs. Nos 20 003 and 20 066 depart from Tinsley Yard with the 9T34 trip working to Sheffield Freight Terminal on 23 September 1980. The load includes KRV, IMX, ILB, RRV, BDO and SPV wagons. *Paul Shannon*

The Skegness branch retained some unusual examples of Great Northern Railway somersault signals in the BR blue period. A five-car DMU comprising Class 114 cars E50039 and E56013 and Class 120 cars M50730, M59283 and M50656 enters Havenhouse station with the 13.44 from Skegness to Nottingham on 1 August 1981. *Paul Shannon*

Approaching the three-way junction at Wrawby, just west of Barnetby, on 1 August 1984 are Nos 31 181 and 31 243 with train 6M57, the 09.55 Lindsey Refinery–Kingsbury oil tanks. The 12-wagon load seems modest compared with the trains of up to 26 bogie tanks that operate out of Lindsey today. The two locomotives pictured were sent for scrap in 1995 and 1990 respectively. *Paul Shannon*

The BR double-arrow symbol lives on in the privatised era: No 08 632 shunts BSA steel wagons at Immingham reception sidings on 29 October 1997. A decade later EWS operates a larger number of Class 08 shunters than any other company, although wherever possible it deploys main-line traction instead. *Paul Shannon*

Doncaster Works specialised in repairing and overhauling English Electric locomotives such as Classes 37, 50 and 55. Pictured receiving attention on 24 April 1977 are Nos 37 211, 37 042, 37 286 and 55 006 *The Fife and Forfar Yeomanry*. *Paul Shannon*

Above:
The use of a telephoto lens foreshortens locomotives 31 245 and 31 191 and their train of empty PGA hoppers as they approach Gilberdyke with train 6M30, the 17.00 from Hull Dairycoates to Rylstone, on 25 July 1984. Both locomotives were allocated to Immingham at that time but would have worked a wide range of freight services across Yorkshire and beyond. *Paul Shannon*

Below:
On 20 July 1990 blue Class 31 No 31 414 pilots large-logo Class 47 No 47 512 on the 12.16 Newcastle–Liverpool Lime Street service, pictured here passing the site of the steam shed at Mirfield. The following year locomotives gave way to second-generation diesel units on trans-Pennine services. No 31 414 later became No 31 514 and survives today on the Ecclesbourne Valley Railway. *Paul Shannon*

Above:
The then recently renumbered Class 25 No 25 056 passes
Heaton Lodge Junction on 14 May 1974 with a westbound train
conveying mainly domestic coal. The four-character headcode
(8M08) allows the train to be identified 33 years later as the
13.45 departure from Healey Mills to Brewery Sidings,
Manchester, which service was also scheduled to call at
Middleton Junction to detach coal for Chadderton.
Gavin Morrison

Below:
The Class 56s were the last BR diesel class to be outshopped
in Rail blue. One of the Romanian-built examples, No 56 020,
passes Milnsbridge with an empty merry-go-round train
from Fiddler's Ferry power station on 23 October 1982.
Gavin Morrison

Holbeck-based Class 45 'Peak' No 33 passes Batley with an early-morning trans-Pennine working on 14 June 1974. This locomotive was not equipped to provide electric train heating and would soon be renumbered into the '45/0' series as No 45 019. *Gavin Morrison*

More than 200 Class 03 shunters were supplied to BR, but by the mid-1970s fewer than 70 examples remained in use, as many of their duties had either been taken over by Class 08s or disappeared altogether. Coupled to its obligatory match wagon to prevent the risk of the short-wheelbase locomotive failing to operate track circuits, No 03 371 is pictured at Bradford Interchange station on 26 April 1977. Today the locomotive lives on at Rowden Mill Station Museum in Herefordshire. *Gavin Morrison*

Top:
Carrying the short-lived livery combination of Rail blue and small yellow warning panels, 'Peak' No D55 *Royal Signals* stands outside Leeds Holbeck shed on 18 March 1967. This locomotive was later renumbered 45 144 and worked expresses on the Midland main line until ousted by InterCity 125 units.
Gavin Morrison

Above:
Early repaints of Class 25 locomotives into Rail blue had double-arrow symbols on the cabside and numbers on the bodyside. Freshly outshopped No D5202 is pictured at Leeds Holbeck depot on 8 June 1967. The locomotive later became No 25 052 and spent its last years on the Western Region before withdrawal in 1980. Holbeck lost its main-line diesel allocation in 1978. *Gavin Morrison*

Top:
Simultaneous departures from York on 11 August 1981: 'Deltic' No 55 021 *Argyll and Sutherland Highlander* **heads the 15.50 York–King's Cross as No 47 486 sets out with a late-running cross-country service. By this time one of the few 'Deltics' to remain in service, No 55 021 would survive until the last day of 'Deltic'-hauled service trains on 31 December 1981.**
Paul Shannon

Above:
With summer Saturday extras from places such as Newcastle and Glasgow, the York–Scarborough line saw a good variety of locomotive-hauled trains in the 1970s. Haymarket-allocated Class 40 No 40 159 follows the valley of the River Derwent near Huttons Ambo with a Scarborough-bound service on 17 July 1976. *Gavin Morrison*

No 40 077 stands in Tees Up Yard at the head of train 6D75, the 16.05 departure to Scunthorpe, on 24 March 1982. By this time the rationalisation of Tees Yard was not far off: the up hump and reception sidings closed in 1982, and the down hump ceased operating three years later, leaving a much-reduced flat shunting facility for residual wagonload and steel traffic. *Paul Shannon*

Left:
With gas lighting still in evidence, a two-car Metropolitan-Cammell DMU departs from Ruswarp station with a train from Darlington and Middlesbrough to Whitby on the afternoon of a pleasant day in March 1969. Soon the line would be singled and the station would be reduced to an unstaffed halt. *Geoff Plumb*

Above:
The line between Middlesbrough and Redcar passed some of
the most impressive industrial scenery on the BR network. The
British Steel coke ovens at South Bank form the backdrop to
this view of Nos 31 292 and 31 178 heading west with a single
Cleveland Potash wagon on 25 March 1982. Two hours of
observation at South Bank on that day were rewarded with
nine freight movements. *Paul Shannon*

Below:
The harsh winter light illuminates No 37 195 as it stands beside
Seabanks 'box before working a coal train from Seaham
Harbour on 6 February 1982. This was before the year-long
miners' strike, which would hasten the already rapid decline
in Britain's coal-mining industry. Seabanks 'box survived
until 1987, when the short branch from Seaham was singled.
In recent years a new rail terminal has been opened on the
former Seaham Harbour branch to receive cement from
Dunbar and Hope. *Paul Shannon*

Above:
No 55 016 *Gordon Highlander* heads north from Durham with the 07.36 cross-country service from Plymouth to Edinburgh on 10 October 1981. The 'Deltic' would have taken over from a Class 47 locomotive at York. By this time most expresses on the East Coast main line were already in the hands of InterCity 125 units, and the few remaining 'Deltic' turns were avidly followed by enthusiasts. *Paul Shannon*

Below:
Springtime at Durham: No 47 551 departs with an up InterCity service on 13 May 1982. New as No D1746, this locomotive was renumbered five times in its 38-year career: first as 47 153, then 47 551, then 47 801, then back to 47 551, and finally as 47 774. It was also allocated at some time or other to all BR regions except the Southern. *Paul Shannon*

One of the early build of 'skinhead' Class 31s without a roof-mounted four-character headcode panel, No 31 134 approaches Plawsworth on the East Coast main line with an up unfitted coal train on 14 May 1982. The locomotive was allocated to Thornaby at the time; it spent most of its life on the Eastern Region but was transferred to Wigan before its withdrawal in 1996. *Paul Shannon*

With the south end of Tyne Yard just visible in the distance, No 47 417 creates a wake of snow as it approaches Birtley with an up express on 12 December 1981. The locomotive entered service in 1963 as No D1516; equipped from new to provide electric train heating, it spent much of its working life on the East Coast main line. *Paul Shannon*

Making a change from the usual diet of DMUs on the Durham Coast line, No 47 091 crosses the High Level Bridge between Newcastle and Gateshead with an additional 13.53 Newcastle–Seaburn football supporters' train on 28 November 1981. *Paul Shannon*

After a brief initial spell on the Western Region, No 37 212 was based at various Eastern Region depots between 1969 and 1987. It is pictured approaching Pelaw with an unfitted coal train for the Leamside line on 1 March 1982. The then recently built tracks of the Tyne & Wear Metro are just visible on the far left. *Paul Shannon*

A small pool of Class 56 locomotives was based at Gateshead for working merry-go-round coal trains in the North East. No 56 080 draws its train forward under the rapid loader at Butterwell opencast disposal point on 17 July 1986. Once fully loaded the train will run forward to Tyne Yard via the East Coast main line. No 56 080 later carried the name *Selby Coalfield*; it was taken out of use in 1999 and scrapped four years later after donating parts for the restoration of other Class 56s. *Paul Shannon*

THREE

London Midland Region

The 'dieselisation' of the London Midland Region had begun as early as 1957, when the first 20 English Electric Type 1s, later known as Class 20, were delivered to Devons Road depot in London. But the diesel takeover was a long process: in the North West of England Stanier Class 5s could still be seen in 1968, working alongside Rail-blue diesels. At the same time diesel traction on West Coast routes from London to Birmingham, Manchester and Liverpool had already given way to electrics.

At the end of 1969 the London Midland Region had members of Classes 20, 24, 25, 40, 44, 45, 46, 47 and 50 on its books. Its last examples of Classes 17, 27 and 28 had recently been transferred away or scrapped, the Metropolitan-Vickers Class 28s having ended their days on secondary services in Cumbria.

The Class 20s were by no means limited to the London Midland Region, but for many years they were staple traction on coal trains in and around the East Midlands, invariably working in pairs. The arrival of BR's second-generation freight diesels of Classes 56 and 58 spelled the beginning of end for the Class 20s, but it was not until 1995, following the introduction of the Class 60s, that the class was retired from main-line use. Even after that they made a comeback with Direct Rail Services, and several can still be seen on the main line today.

The Sulzer-engined, BR-designed Classes 24 and 25 were widely used on the London Midland Region throughout the BR blue period. They worked a range of freight duties, both singly and in pairs, and passenger trains including scheduled services on the Marches line via Shrewsbury as well as excursions and dated holiday trains. Class 24 withdrawals started in the late 1960s, and the bulk of the fleet was withdrawn between 1975 and 1979, just one example surviving until October 1980. The Class 25s lasted rather longer, withdrawals not gathering pace until the 1980s; the last Class 25s were taken out of service in 1987. More than 20 examples of the two classes have been preserved.

The English Electric Class 40s were a characteristic sight on freight and passenger duties in North West England in the Rail-blue period. In later years their lack of electric train-heating equipment precluded them from most passenger work; all were withdrawn by the end of 1986 except for celebrity machine No 40 122, which was restored to green livery and worked on the main line for two more years. Seven Class 40s still exist today in preservation.

The Class 44 and 45 'Peaks' were closely associated with the Midland main line from the end of steam until the arrival of InterCity 125s in the 1980s. The Pilot Scheme Class 44s were largely restricted to freight work in the East Midlands from 1962 until their withdrawal between 1976 and 1980, while the Class 45s were divided in the mid-1970s into two sub-classes — Class 45/1 (with electric train heating) for InterCity use and Class 45/0 (initially retaining steam-heating boilers) for non-ETH passenger work and freight. The last Class 45 was retired from normal service in 1988. The Class 46 'Peaks' also worked on the London Midland Region but mainly on the North East–South West axis; the last example was withdrawn in 1984. More than a dozen 'Peaks' survive in preservation.

The Brush Class 47s constituted BR's most numerous diesel class and were often dismissed by enthusiasts until the introduction of second-generation diesel units made the sight of any locomotive-hauled passenger train rare. They certainly covered a wide geographical spread and were no more London Midland engines than they were Eastern, Western or, in later years, Scottish. Several examples remain in traffic at the time of writing, although their days of regular operation on what had been the InterCity network ended in 2002.

Although they worked on the London Midland Region for less than a decade, the English Electric Class 50s made a big impression on the northern half of the West Coast main line until displaced by electrics in 1974. While on the London Midland they were allocated to only one depot, Crewe, and carried only one livery — BR blue.

Above:
The delivery of the Class 25 fleet was not completed until 1967, and the last 18 examples carried Rail blue from new. One of that final batch, No D7666, is pictured at Willesden on 9 April 1967. It was renumbered 25 316 under the TOPS scheme and was further renumbered 25 911 in 1986 as a member of the short-lived Chemicals & Industrial Minerals pool based at Crewe.
John Feild

Below:
Still carrying its original blue livery, No 56 004 passes South Kenton with the 15.00 Willesden–Mossend 'Enterprise' wagonload service on 26 July 1995. At this time the Class 56 fleet was split between the Transrail and Loadhaul freight companies, the Transrail machines being shared between Cardiff Canton and Motherwell depots. *Paul Shannon*

Above:
The forlorn single-platform terminus at St Albans Abbey is pictured on 21 August 1979, with Cravens Class 105 cars M56482, M50391, M50387 and M56148 forming the shuttle service to Watford Junction. The St Albans Abbey branch was electrified in 1988, but the terminus is still an unstaffed halt with only a basic shelter for passengers. *Paul Shannon*

Below:
A pair of four-car Class 127 units forming a Luton–St Pancras working call at West Hampstead Midland station on 6 April 1978. Of non-standard design, the Class 127s spent their entire lives on the St Pancras–Bedford route, finally bowing out in 1983 after electrification had been commissioned. *Paul Shannon*

Above:
'Peaks' equipped to supply electric train heating were classified '45/1' under the TOPS scheme. Allocated to Toton, they were the mainstay of InterCity services on the Midland main line until InterCity 125 units took over in the early 1980s. No 45 109 approaches St Albans with an up train comprising Mk 1 stock on 11 August 1979. *Paul Shannon*

Below:
Newspaper traffic was still an important source of revenue for BR in the 1970s, especially on routes out of London. Class 45 'Peak' No 45 110 passes the site of Chiltern Green station, south of Luton, with empty newspaper vans on 19 September 1978. The locomotive was built with split headcode panels, but these had been removed before this photograph was taken. *Paul Shannon*

Above:
The last Class 50 to be repainted in BR blue livery after refurbishment was No 50 013 *Agincourt,* **released from Doncaster Works in 1980. It was also the last member of the class to receive large-logo livery, in 1984. Towards the end of its time in BR blue, on 7 April 1983, it passes Fenny Compton with the 11.20 Liverpool Lime Street–Paddington service.**
Paul Shannon

Below:
A Derby suburban DMU, later designated Class 116, passes Acocks Green on the 12.50pm Birmingham Snow Hill–Lapworth local service on 1 March 1967. By this time the former GWR lines around Birmingham had been transferred to London Midland Region control, but Western Region lower-quadrant signalling remained in use. *Michael Mensing*

Above:
One of the last half dozen Class 24s to remain in service was No 24 047. It is pictured on 2 September 1978, shortly before its withdrawal, backing a train of track panels into Small Heath sidings on the former GWR approach to Birmingham.
Michael Mensing

Below:
Class 45 'Peak' No 74 passes Anglesea Sidings, on the Lichfield–Walsall line, with a southbound mixed freight on the evening of 30 May 1974. The adjacent bitumen sidings have just had a delivery of tanks brought in by No 47 043, visible in the distance. This line closed as a through route in 1984.
Michael Mensing

Above:
No 25 245 stands in the bay platform at Shrewsbury on 13 May 1982 with a short parcels train for Birmingham New Street, comprising BR standard General Utility Van No W86218 and a BR standard Covered Carriage Truck. *John Feild*

Below:
With GWR pattern lower quadrant signals much in evidence, 'Crompton' No 33 063 approaches Shrewsbury station with the 16.02 Crewe–Cardiff Central service on 10 August 1982. Towards the end of its BR career No 33 063 became a dedicated freight machine and was repainted in Trainload Construction livery; it was later purchased and restored to working order by the South East Locomotive Group. *Paul Shannon*

Above:
Wagonload freight on the Cambrian Coast line hung on by a thread in the 1970s, explosives traffic from Penrhyndeudraeth, along with occasional deliveries of coal, providing the main source of revenue. On 26 September 1978 No 25 325 enters Harlech station with one empty CXV van for Penrhyndeudraeth, one MCO mineral wagon with coal from Gwaun-cae-Gurwen to Porthmadog and one MCV mineral wagon with coal from Gwaun-cae-Gurwen to Pwllheli.
Paul Shannon

Below:
Shortly after its conversion to an ETH-fitted Class 31/4, Cricklewood-based No 31 422 pilots Class 25 No 25 254 on a merry-go-round coal train from Thoresby colliery to Northfleet cement works on 22 April 1975. The location is Glendon Junction, where the branch from Corby joins the Midland main line. *Hugh Ballantyne*

Many Class 20s retained BR blue livery into the 1990s. Nos 20 166 and 20 081 await the right of way from Toton Up Yard with train 6E98, the 19.18 departure to Seymour, on 17 July 1989. No 20 166 was withdrawn by BR in 1991 but then worked on Channel Tunnel construction trains until its purchase by the Bodmin & Wenford Railway in 1993. *Paul Shannon*

Above:
This heterogeneous line-up at Toton depot on 8 July 1976 includes members of Classes 20, 47, 44, 45 and 40. At that time Toton had an allocation of more than 270 main-line locomotives, a larger number than any other BR depot. *Gavin Morrison*

Be;ow:
The Drewry 'D22xx' shunter design survived long enough to be given a TOPS designation, Class 04, but all examples were withdrawn before the 1974 renumbering scheme. A rare blue-liveried example, No D2209, is pictured at Derby shed on 10 May 1967. *John Feild*

Above:
The 9T40 headcode denotes an unfitted trip working as smartly repainted No 25 206 stands beside Engine Sidings No 2 'box at Derby on 16 June 1974. Although the main line through Derby had been resignalled in 1969, Engine Sidings No 2 'box survived to control access to the motive power depot until the late 1980s.
Hugh Ballantyne

Below:
The 10 'Peaks' ordered under the 1955 Modernisation Plan's Pilot Scheme were later designated Class 44. Originally mixed-traffic locomotives, they soon found themselves restricted to freight duties in the East Midlands. No 44 003 *Skiddaw* passes Trowell, near Ilkeston, with an up unfitted coal train on 17 September 1975. Withdrawals of the class began the following year, and the type became extinct on BR in 1980.
Hugh Ballantyne

Above:

The former steam shed at Westhouses lived on as a diesel stabling point until the closure of most of the local collieries left it without a purpose. Nos 20 161 and 20 148 are parked up outside the shed on 31 December 1981. The locomotives' engines had been left running over the New Year holiday period, perhaps to prevent frost damage or perhaps just because they could not be relied upon to start again. The characteristic whistle could be heard some distance away, drifting across the snow-covered landscape. *Stewart Jolly*

Below:

No 45 015 passes Alfreton & Mansfield Parkway station with an up train of 30 MXV mineral wagons on 24 July 1984. By that time BR had abandoned its vacuum-braked wagonload network, but vacuum-braked wagons were still plentiful on block workings such as this. No 45 015 was withdrawn from Toton depot in 1986 and then dumped out of use until its move to the Battlefield Line at Shackerstone in 2002. *Paul Shannon*

Hauling a mixture of BR maroon and blue-and-grey Mk 1 stock, 'Peak' No D114 passes Clay Cross with the up 'Thames–Clyde Express' on 21 August 1967. The locomotive was later renumbered 45 066 but ended its working life as No 97 413, one of a small pool of former Class 45s dedicated to infrastructure trains. *John Feild*

After closure of the Buxton–Matlock line in 1968 BR rerouted its Manchester–Derby–St Pancras services via the Hope Valley and Chesterfield. 'Peak' No 45 022 *Lytham St Annes*, formerly No D60, approaches Grindleford station with an up working for St Pancras on 26 March 1981. BR later withdrew this re-routed service, although it made a temporary return in 2003/4 whilst the West Coast main line was disrupted by engineering blockades. *Paul Shannon*

No 40 099 passes Edale with the 6T38 trip working from Earle's Sidings to Dewsnap on 26 March 1981, conveying CPV Presflo wagons for distribution by the wagonload network. At that time the locomotive still had its nose-end doors, but marker lights had replaced the four white discs that were originally fitted to identify the category of train. *Paul Shannon*

Above:
For more than 30 years Buxton depot maintained a fleet of Class 104 DMUs for the local service to Manchester. Two units are pictured inside the shed on 14 April 1977. Second-generation 'Sprinter' units took over the service from 1989, and the depot closed a few years later, once a replacement fuelling point for freight locomotives had been installed at Peak Forest. *Paul Shannon*

Below:
Single Class 25s took over from steam on the famous Tunstead–Oakleigh limestone trains and remained in charge until the 1980s. No 25 161 accelerates away from Great Rocks Junction with train 6F44, the 17.45 departure from Tunstead, on 7 July 1983. The bogie hopper wagons, some of which dated back to the 1930s, remained in service until 1997. *Paul Shannon*

Above:
In the 1974 renumbering scheme the Class 47s were divided into three sub-classes: 47/0 for locomotives with steam train-heating equipment, 47/3 for those with no train-heating equipment and 47/4 for those with electric or dual train-heating equipment. Many Class 47/3s worked merry-go-round trains until replaced by Classes 56 and 58. At Stafford on 21 August 1979 Class 47/3 No 47 326 heads south with 30 HAA hoppers, likely to have been bound for Ironbridge. *Paul Shannon*

Below:
The LMS-design diesel shunters retained their five-digit 1948 numbers until withdrawal. A few examples survived long enough to receive BR blue livery. No 12062 is pictured at Crewe Works on 28 April 1968. *John Edgington*

Above:
The Class 50s were the first complete class of BR diesel locomotives to be outshopped in blue livery. Brand-new No D421 is pictured at Crewe Works on 28 April 1968. The locomotive had not yet been fitted with its multiple-control jumper cables, which would be required when regular double-heading commenced on the West Coast main line.
John Edgington

Below:
Although allocated to the Trainload Coal sub-sector No 37 139 was rostered on 26 May 1990 for train 1V03, the 14.23 Bolton–Cardiff Central parcels and mail. It seems to be attracting a fair amount of interest as it pulls away from Crewe; the normal diesel traction for parcels trains at that time was a Class 31 or 47.
Paul Shannon

The Freightliner network was originally geared to domestic and short-sea traffic, in contrast to the almost 100% reliance on deep-sea business today. Large numbers of containers were moved to and from Ireland via Holyhead. With a matching rake of Freightliner containers in tow, No 40 174 passes Calveley with the 12.00 Holyhead–Willesden service on 20 June 1976. *John Feild*

In the 1970s the North Wales Coast line produced numerous locomotive-hauled workings on summer Saturdays. No 40 170 leaves Chester with the 09.18 Manchester Victoria–Rhyl service on 22 June 1974. The locomotive shows the final variation in Class 40 front-end design — a central four-digit headcode panel with no inter-connecting doors. *John Feild*

Above:
A regular Class 08 duty was the trip working between Dee Marsh Junction sidings and the Shotton Paper private siding, conveying timber from Scotland and, in later years, finished paper products in both directions between Shotton and Irvine. No 08 894 propels OTA wagons with logs from Stirling into the Shotton plant on 9 July 1991. *Paul Shannon*

Below:
Pairs of Class 25s could still occasionally be seen on passenger workings in the early 1980s, even though the class was rapidly heading for extinction. Nos 25 153 and 25 221 pull away from Rhyl with the combined service from York (09.00) and Sheffield (08.57) to Llandudno on 14 August 1982. *Paul Shannon*

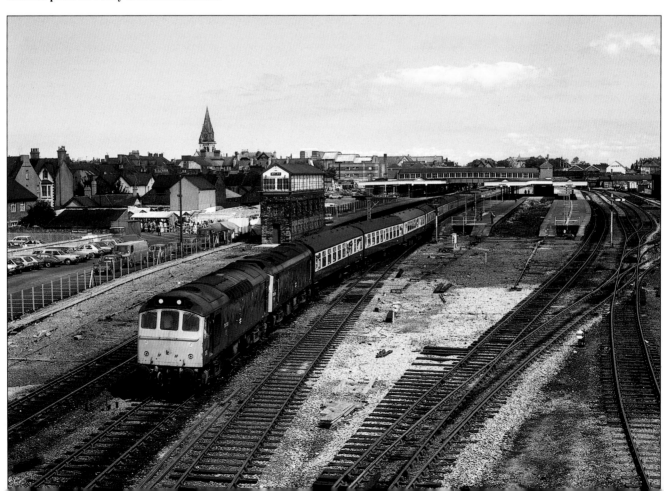

Above:
No 47 544 runs alongside the A55 road at Mochdre, between Colwyn Bay and Llandudno Junction, with the 13.00 Cardiff Central–Holyhead service on 10 August 1987. Delivered new to the Western Region as No D1592 in 1964, the locomotive spent much of its career working from Eastern Region depots. It was withdrawn prematurely in 1990 following fire damage. *Paul Shannon*

Below:
The London Midland Region regained a small allocation of Class 03 shunters to handle a temporary upturn in freight traffic at Birkenhead Docks. No 03 189 shunts CGV grain hoppers from Chettisham into the Rank private siding at Birkenhead on 6 July 1983. After withdrawal by BR the shunter was moved to the Ribble Steam Railway, where it is undergoing restoration at the time of writing. *Paul Shannon*

Above:
The Gloucester Carriage & Wagon Co produced a total of 40 two-car DMU sets for the Scottish and London Midland regions, although some were later transferred to the Eastern Region. Under the TOPS scheme they were designated Class 100. Driving trailer No 56103 is nearest the camera in this view of Longsight depot on 25 February 1979. *Gavin Morrison*

Below:
No 47 194 passes Ordsall Lane Junction with train 4D59, the 15.54 Trafford Park–Holyhead Freightliner working, on 28 May 1985. This train followed a circuitous route from Trafford Park via Chorlton-cum-Hardy, Ashburys, Miles Platting and Manchester Victoria. At the time of writing No 47 194 is stored out of use at Carnforth in the ownership of West Coast Railways. *Paul Shannon*

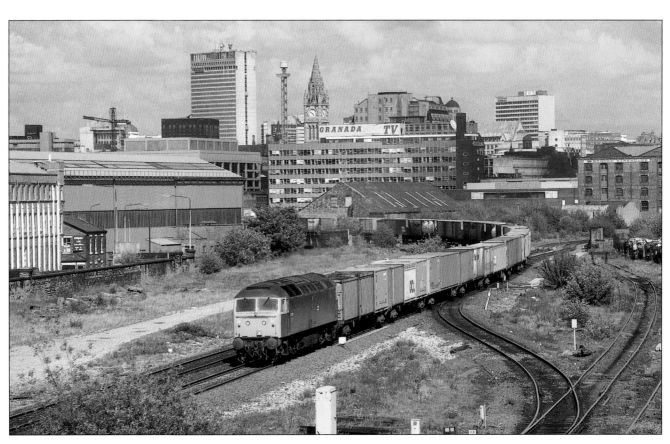

Above:
BR once carried oil in both directions across the Pennines — from Stanlow to destinations in Yorkshire and the North East and from Immingham and Teesside to destinations in the North West. No 40 126 whistles gently into Manchester Victoria with a westbound tank train on 25 July 1979. *Paul Shannon*

Below:
The railway landscape of Bolton was set to change dramatically soon after this photograph was taken, with the semaphores giving way to colour lights and the goods warehouse facing demolition before redevelopment. No 47 613 *North Star* departs on 29 May 1984 with the combined service from Edinburgh (11.10) and Glasgow Central (11.20) to Harwich Parkeston Quay while No 45 051 shunts the local steel terminal.
Paul Shannon

Class 31s appeared both singly and in multiple on commuter trains from Manchester to Southport and Blackpool. Nos 31 438 and 31 442 call at Wigan Wallgate with the 17.30 from Manchester Victoria to Southport on 6 July 1992. The use of early Mk 2 stock gave passengers a welcome change from the first-generation DMUs that had recently been phased out. *Paul Shannon*

Still in obsolete blue livery, albeit faded, Nos 20 045 and 20 159 stand at the head of a merry-go-round train at Bickershaw on 7 June 1989, carrying coal for Fiddler's Ferry power station. At that time Bickershaw had no run-round loop, and all trains on the branch were 'topped and tailed', in this case with two Class 20s at each end. *Paul Shannon*

One of the last 30 or so Class 47s to retain BR blue livery, No 47 270, heads north at Winwick Junction with train 6Z17, the 14.35 Widnes–Lindsey empty tanks, on 12 July 1991. The bodyside nameplate *Swift* had been applied unofficially at its home depot, Tinsley. *Paul Shannon*

In order to achieve accelerated timings between Crewe and Glasgow, from 1970 Class 50s were diagrammed to work in pairs on certain services. In this 29 May 1971 view Nos 422 and 445 pass Carnforth with the 13.45 Glasgow Central–Euston. *John Edgington*

Above:
In the mid-1980s the Little North Western route between Carnforth and Skipton saw a temporary return to locomotive-hauled operation, replacing 'Inter-City' DMUs which had themselves been cascaded from other routes. No 31 440 is pictured near Clapham with the 13.36 from Lancaster to Hull on 9 June 1984. *Paul Shannon*

Below:
The Settle–Carlisle line was heavily used by wagonload freight trains which would have been too slow for the West Coast main line. Class 25 No D7673 momentarily shatters the peace of the snow-covered landscape as it passes Horton-in-Ribblesdale with a Carlisle-bound train on 7 February 1970. The consist includes Prestwin bulk powder wagons and Conflat wagons with 'L' containers, which were used to carry dolomite. *Gavin Morrison*

Above:
In 1970 the Settle–Carlisle line lost its local passenger trains and the two remaining intermediate stations, Settle and Appleby, were left with a sparse InterCity service. No 40 105 enters Appleby station with the afternoon train to Nottingham on 13 January 1979. The through Nottingham service was withdrawn in 1982, and it looked as if worse was to come. Happily S&C supporters won their high-profile campaign for a reprieve, and today the line is again busy with both freight and passengers. *Paul Shannon*

Below:
The Class 50s spent barely seven years on their intended duties on the West Coast main line before being displaced by electrification and cascaded to the Western Region. Just before the electrification project was authorised, No D445 passes Shap Summit with an up express on 7 March 1970.
Gavin Morrison

Above:
The unique Metropolitan-Vickers Co-Bo design, later known
as Class 28, was one of the undoubted failures of the 1955
Modernisation Plan. The 20 locomotives entered service in 1958
but were disastrously unreliable, and all were withdrawn by the
end of 1968. Just one example, No D5701, received blue livery;
it is pictured near Grange-over-Sands hauling empty Fina tanks
from Whitehaven to Heysham Moss on 21 June 1968. Another
member of the class, No D5705, survived against all the odds
as a departmental locomotive and is now preserved on the
East Lancashire Railway. *Michael Mensing*

Below:
The Cumbrian Coast line retained a variety of freight workings
in the 1980s and even enjoyed a Travelling Post Office service
to and from Workington. On 30 July 1985 No 47 466 rounds
the curve at Parton with train 4P24, the 17.53 departure
from Workington to Preston. This train became 1P24 from
Whitehaven and continued from Preston as 1E01, the 23.09
to Huddersfield. *Paul Shannon*

Above:
Although the Class 17 'Claytons' were mainly Scottish locomotives, a number worked in West Cumberland. Nos D8506 and D8500 approach Workington with a southbound freight on 20 June 1968. Both locomotives were withdrawn by the end of that year. *Michael Mensing*

Below:
In their early days the Class 50s worked freight as well as passenger trains on the West Coast main line. With a Derby lightweight DMU stabled on one of the centre roads, No D427 departs Carlisle station after a brief stop with a Glasgow–London (York Way) Freightliner on 28 June 1968.
Michael Mensing

FOUR

Southern Region

On much of the Southern Region network steam traction gave way directly to electric as BR continued the third-rail policy of the Southern Railway. Even the Bournemouth line hung on to steam until its third rail was energised in 1967. Nevertheless, diesel locomotives were required for non-electrified lines, for inter-regional trains and for freight duties requiring access to non-electrified sidings. In 1969 the two depots at Eastleigh and Hither Green shared an allocation of 96 Birmingham Railway Carriage & Wagon Co Class 33s, divided into three sub-classes: the standard Class 33/0 version, Class 33/1 with push-pull equipment for the Weymouth line, and Class 33/2 with narrow body profile for the Hastings line. The Region also operated Class 73 and Class 74 electro-diesels, the latter having been converted from Class 71 electrics.

Aside from its main-line fleet the Southern Region was home to most of the Class 09 shunters, which differed from the Class 08s in having high-level air pipes for coupling to electric units as well as a higher maximum speed of 27mph. For local services on non-electrified lines the Southern opted for diesel-electric instead of diesel-mechanical multiple-units, mainly to achieve maximum commonality with its fleet of electric multiple-units.

The Class 33 locomotives remained based on the Southern Region throughout the Rail-blue period, although in the 1980s their duties took them regularly as far as West Wales and North West England. Accident victims aside, the first withdrawals did not occur until 1985, and more than 20 members of the class remain active today, either on preserved lines or on the national network. The versatile Class 73 electro-diesels have also stood the test of time, several examples still serving GB Railfreight and other operators in the 21st century.

Although the Class 33s and electro-diesels were the only locomotives allocated to the Southern Region in the 1970s and 1980s, inter-regional trains brought a variety of other types, notably (in the early 1970s) the Class 42 and Class 43 'Warships', as well as Classes 31, 47 and 50.

The 9½-mile branch from Appledore to Lydd Town lost its passenger service in 1967 but survives today for nuclear flask traffic to and from Dungeness power station. One of the Hastings 'slim line' Class 33s, No 33 206, is pictured on the branch with the inward flask train on 25 August 1983. At that time all the flask trains required barrier wagons — former BR-owned ferry vans on this occasion — and a brake van. *Paul Shannon*

Above:
Class 09 shunters had a long association with the train-ferry operation at Dover. No 09 022 shunts Interfrigo vans at Hawkesbury Street Junction, Dover, on 27 August 1977. It is sad that no perishables traffic travels by rail today between Britain and mainland Europe, despite the shorter journey times that ought to be possible thanks to the Channel Tunnel. *Michael Mensing*

Below:
The building of the Channel Tunnel produced a number of additional short-term freight flows on the Southern Region, including concrete lining segments from Grain and minestone shale from Snowdown. No 33 047 has just emerged from Shakespeare Tunnel on the approach to Dover with shale empties from Sevington to Snowdown on 22 August 1989.
Paul Shannon

Above:

Transrail-operated No 56 004 departs Sheerness with the 11.10 'Enterprise' feeder service to Willesden on 24 July 1995, carrying wire rod for distribution to Blackburn and Mossend. One of the last two operational Class 56s to retain BR blue livery, No 56 004 was withdrawn from Immingham in 1999 and scrapped in 2006. *Paul Shannon*

Below:

Class 50s took over many Waterloo–Exeter services in 1980 and remained in charge until replaced by Class 159 units in the early 1990s. No 50 011 *Centurion* passes Wimbledon with an Exeter-bound service on 21 September 1981. The locomotive was withdrawn from service in 1987 and scrapped at Crewe in 1992 after a period in suspended animation as a static engine testbed. *Paul Shannon*

The plume of exhaust shows that electro-diesel No 73 116 is working in diesel mode as it leaves Tolworth with train 7V45, the 10.23 coal empties to Acton, on 22 August 1983. At that time the Class 73s were diagrammed for a range of freight and passenger services, including inter-regional workings to Willesden as well as Acton. No 73 116 was later named *Selhurst* and renumbered 73 210 as a dedicated 'Gatwick Express' locomotive. *Paul Shannon*

Specifically designed for the tight curvature of lines in Southampton Docks, a fleet of 14 shunters (later Class 07) was introduced in 1962 to replace 'USA' 0–6–0 tank engines. Unfortunately the reign of the '07s' was shortened by BR's decision to pull out of wagonload traffic in the docks in the early 1970s. Some were withdrawn in 1973, and the remainder had gone by 1977. No 07 002 is pictured out of use at Eastleigh on 1 October 1977. *John Feild*

Until the 1990s the Class 09 fleet was concentrated on the Southern Region. On 14 August 1990 No 09 025 shunts BDA wagons loaded with imported steel bar at Hamworthy Quay. Despite its freight use the locomotive carries a Network SouthEast logo as well as the unofficial name *Victory*. It remained in use with Connex until 2005 and then passed into preservation on the East Kent Railway. *Paul Shannon*

In order to allow through-running to Weymouth after completion of the London–Bournemouth electrification scheme in 1967, BR converted 19 Class 33s to operate in push-pull mode with '4-TC' trailer units. Freshly repainted locomotive No D6532 hauls a pair of '4-TCs' through the Dorset countryside near Moreton on 2 July 1967. The locomotive later became No 33 114 and survived in main-line use until 1993. *Derek Cross*

Right:
Work-stained Class 31 No 31 293 arrives at Salisbury with the 11.19 Bristol–Portsmouth service on 10 September 1977. The locomotive was later transferred to the London Midland Region and was withdrawn in 1990. *Hugh Ballantyne*

Left:
No 33 002 passes Hanging Langford in the picturesque Wylye Valley with the 13.10 from Portsmouth Harbour to Bristol Temple Meads on 21 August 1987. The passenger service on this route went over to 'Sprinter' operation in the following year, but there would be further spells of locomotive operation, including the use of Fragonset Class 31s in the early 2000s. *Paul Shannon*

Below:
The Southern Region went its own way by ordering a fleet of diesel-electric (instead of diesel-mechanical) multiple-units. Class 205 'Hampshire' unit No 1101 calls at Warminster with a northbound stopping train on 15 April 1978. This unit was later renumbered 205 001 and has since been preserved on the East Kent Railway. *Michael Mensing*

FIVE

Western Region

When the BR corporate image was launched in the mid-1960s the Western Region was already doubting the wisdom of its traction policy, a policy which had seen the building of some 219 diesel-hydraulics between 1958 and 1964 when all other BR regions had opted for diesel-electrics. Although the hydraulics had their strong points, notably their high power-to-weight ratio, the fact that they were non-standard condemned them to early withdrawal.

Among the first hydraulics to go were the five Pilot Scheme 'D6xx' 'Warships', which, as well as being non-standard, had given more than their fair share of trouble and were expensive to maintain. The class was withdrawn *en bloc* in December 1967. The next victims were the 'D63xx' 'Baby Warships', later known as Class 22. They did not perform particularly well, and much of their work disappeared because of the closure of branch lines and the withdrawal of pick-up freights. The class became extinct in 1972. No members of these two classes survived into preservation.

The demise of the other hydraulic classes — the Class 35 'Hymeks', the Class 42 and Class 43 'Warships' and the Class 52 'Westerns' — was primarily a question of BR implementing its 1967 policy of standardisation, of making the Western Region fall into line with the rest of the system. The three Pilot Scheme Class 42 'Warships' were withdrawn in 1968, and the remainder of Classes 42 and 43 were taken out of service by the end of 1972, just two examples surviving into preservation. All but eight of these locomotives had ended their days in blue livery, and in their later years they could be seen working from Old Oak Common, Newton Abbot and Laira depots.

The Class 35 'Hymeks' were the next hydraulics to be eliminated, being withdrawn between October 1971 and March 1975. Ultimately 87 of the 101 Hymeks carried blue livery, but none was renumbered under the TOPS system. The class worked on many parts of the Western Region and in 1970 was shared between Old Oak Common, Bristol Bath Road and Cardiff Canton depots. Four 'Hymeks' have eluded the scrapyard.

The Class 52 'Westerns' were the last hydraulics to roll off the production line and also the last to face withdrawal. As late as spring 1973 the class was intact and still performing front-rank duties on the West of England main line, having been concentrated at Laira depot during 1971. The life of the 'Westerns' was extended well beyond the original withdrawal target of 1974 because of problems with the Class 50s and delays in the commissioning of the High Speed Train (later InterCity 125); the last five examples survived until February 1977, by which time they were unique on the main line in retaining their pre-TOPS numbers on cast bodyside plates. Enthusiast interest in the 'Westerns' was considerable, and seven examples have been preserved.

While the loss of the hydraulics marked the end of a short but significant era, one of the replacement diesel-electric types — Class 50 — became no less of a cult locomotive once established on the Western Region. Although designed for the London Midland Region, the 50 Class 50s spent most of their working lives on the Western, using their 100mph capability to good effect on expresses between Paddington and the West Country, South Wales and Birmingham. Their blue livery was, however, short-lived: the so-called large-logo style was adopted from 1980, and many later received Network SouthEast colours. More than a third of the class survive today in preservation.

Working alongside the distinctive hydraulics and Class 50s in the BR blue period were a wide range of other diesel classes either based at Western Region depots or working regularly on Western Region lines. Special mention must go to the Class 37s, which held a virtual monopoly on coal trains in the South Wales valleys from the end of steam until the early 1990s and which also became characteristic haulage for Cornish china-clay workings.

Above:
Carrying the short-lived combination of Rail-blue livery and small yellow warning panels, Class 52 'Western' No D1036 *Western Emperor* stands outside Old Oak Common shed on 9 April 1967. Although the 'Westerns' would continue to be daily visitors to the capital, in their later years all would be allocated to Plymouth Laira depot for maintenance. *John Feild*

Below:
Class 42 'Warship' No 818 *Glory* stands on display at Swindon Works open day on 13 September 1975, some three years after its retirement. The B-B 'Warships' (later Classes 42 and 43) entered service between 1958 and 1962, but all were withdrawn by the end of 1972. No 818 was finally cut up in 1985. *Hugh Ballantyne*

Above:
One of the original ETH-fitted Class 31s, No 31 415,
arrives at Aylesbury station with train 6M18, the 10.20
Akeman Street–Bletchley fertiliser empties, on 19 August 1989.
This Saturdays-only train followed an unusual route:
it reversed from Akeman Street to Grendon Underwood
Junction, ran locomotive-first to Aylesbury and then returned
north via Grendon Underwood to Bletchley. *Paul Shannon*

Below:
Class 56 locomotives started appearing on merry-go-round
coal trains from the Midlands to Didcot power station in 1978.
One of the Romanian-built examples, No 56 006, heads south
through Oxford with a 45-wagon MGR set on Saturday
2 May 1981. On the adjacent track is a Birmingham-bound
cross-country service hauled by No 47 560. *Paul Shannon*

Top:
The Class 50s became regular traction for inter-city trains on the Reading-Banbury-Birmingham line. No 50 024 *Vanguard* passes Banbury North signalbox with the 11.20 Liverpool Lime Street–Paddington service on 17 April 1982. Like many Class 50s No 50 024 was later repainted in Network SouthEast livery. Withdrawn in February 1991, it was promptly cut up at Old Oak Common. *Paul Shannon*

Above:
In the 1960s a small number of Western Region Class 47s were named after figures representing strength and power. No 47 082 *Atlas* emerges from Middle Hill Tunnel, Box, with a down express on 26 August 1975. Originally built as No D1667, it was subsequently renumbered 47 626 and 47 750. It moved away from the Western Region in 1990 and worked for Rail Express Systems and Virgin Trains before withdrawal in 2000. *Hugh Ballantyne*

Above:

Between 1973 and 1976 BR transferred all 50 Class 50s from the London Midland to the Western Region; here they were put to work on top-link expresses out of Paddington, although they soon gave way to InterCity 125 units on the Bristol and South Wales services. No 50 049 *Defiance* heads east from Bath with a Weston-super-Mare–Paddington train on 26 August 1975. A significant number of Class 50s survive in preservation, and No 50 049 is one of the more active examples, based at Cardiff Canton at the time of writing and authorised to run on the national network. *Hugh Ballantyne*

Below:

The Class 35 'Hymeks' suffered a fate similar to that of the other Western Region diesel-hydraulics, being withdrawn well short of their expected lifespan. No D7081 passes Saltford with train 8O63, the 12.55 Severn Tunnel Junction–Norwood mixed goods, on 11 March 1971. Eighteen 'Hymeks' were withdrawn in 1971, and a further 75 in the following year, their duties being taken over by diesel-electrics, including Classes 25 and 31. *Hugh Ballantyne*

Above:
No 47 513 heads an up mixed goods train at Magor, near Severn Tunnel Junction, on 30 July 1977. This locomotive, formerly numbered D1959, was one of only nine Class 47s delivered new in blue (rather than green) livery. It was based at various Western Region depots between 1972 and 1989 but ended its working days allocated to the Parcels sector at Crewe.
Hugh Ballantyne

Below:
Supplied for the Southern Region between 1960 and 1962, the 98 Class 33 'Cromptons' rarely strayed far from their home territory for the best part of 20 years, but in 1981 they found regular employment on the Marches line between Crewe and Cardiff, taking over from Class 25s. No 33 024 approaches Dinmore Tunnel with the 08.00 departure from Cardiff Central on 9 August 1982. *Paul Shannon*

Top:
With the single-track Central Wales Line diverging to the left, No 25 063 leaves Craven Arms station with the 16.00 Crewe–Cardiff service in perfect weather on 1 October 1977. The Class 25s had only recently taken over Marches line duties from Swindon 'Cross-Country' diesel multiple-units.
Hugh Ballantyne

Above:
One of the last four 'Hymeks' to remain in service was No 7017, which finally bowed out in March 1975 after just 13 years on the main line. Cardiff General is the location for this view recorded on 25 January 1975. Happily the locomotive was saved by preservationists and at the time of writing is based on the West Somerset Railway. *John Feild*

Radyr was the focal point for coal traffic in the Cardiff valleys, with a daily schedule of more than 100 trip workings to and from local mines and other freight locations in the 1970s. An unidentified Class 37 waits for the road into Radyr Yard with a trainload of HTV hoppers from Trehafod in July 1977. The DMU on the up platform line carries the then new white-and-blue livery for refurbished stock. *Michael Rhodes*

The Class 37s became staple traction on South Wales coal trains after the demise of steam and remained in charge for the best part of three decades. Returning to Margam after hauling a trainload of coal up the valley to Ogmore, No 37 234 passes Tondu with a solitary brake van on 15 April 1982. The locomotive had been delivered new to the Western Region in 1964 as No D6934.
Paul Shannon

Above:
Loose-coupled coal trains remained a feature of South Wales operations throughout the 'BR blue' period. No 37 159 approaches Burrows Sidings with a rake of MCO mineral wagons from Swansea Docks on 23 August 1978. This locomotive was particularly well travelled, being based at various times on the Western, Scottish, Eastern, London Midland and Southern regions. In 1988 it was fitted with re-geared CP7 bogies and renumbered 37 372.
Hugh Ballantyne

Below:
The use of triple-headed Class 03 locomotives on the Cwmmawr branch was a remarkable survival in the 1980s. Nos 03 144, 03 151 and 03 120 are pictured between Kidwelly and Burry Port with coal from Cwmmawr on 15 September 1983, shortly before the closure of this section of the line. A total of eight Class 03s had been adapted for use on the branch, with reduced-height cabs because of the low bridges and headlights for the open crossings; they were later replaced by Class 08 shunters which also had specially cut-down cabs. *Michael Rhodes*

Westbury was still a feast of lower-quadrant semaphores when No 33 031 was photographed arriving with the 12.14 from Bristol Temple Meads to Portsmouth Harbour on 29 July 1982. Soon the semaphores would give way to multiple-aspect signalling, while No 33 031 would soldier on until succumbing to fire damage in 1989. *Paul Shannon*

Above:
Class 35 'Hymek' No D7033 takes the Westbury line at Fairwood Junction with a rake of HTV hopper wagons on 12 July 1969. Although still bearing the legend 'HOUSE COAL CONCENTRATION' these wagons had been reallocated to aggregates traffic from Merehead Quarry following a sharp decline in the household-coal business. *Hugh Ballantyne*

Below:
The 'Westerns' had regular freight as well as passenger duties. No D1005 *Western Venturer* roars past Fairwood Junction with a down goods train off the Westbury line on 19 August 1972. At that time the fleet of 'Westerns' was still intact, but the first withdrawals would take place during 1973, and four years after that the class would be extinct on BR. *Hugh Ballantyne*

The most numerous main-line diesel built for BR, the Class 47 was also highly versatile, handling every type of train from express passenger to local trip freight. On 29 August 1970 No 1595 arrives at Chilmark RAF siding, west of Salisbury, with a short vacuum-braked freight working, including large and small variants of the 'door to door' containers that had paved the way for Freightliner in the 1960s. No 1595 was renumbered 47 469 in 1974, in which year it moved to Scotland. It was withdrawn in 1989. *Hugh Ballantyne*

Regular duties for the 'Warships' included passenger trains on the downgraded ex-London & South Western Railway line between Waterloo and Exeter. No D827 *Kelly* leaves Gillingham with the 08.50 departure from Exeter on 29 August 1970. The following year would see most 'Warships' dispatched to the scrapyard. *Hugh Ballantyne*

Class 33s took over Waterloo–Exeter services from the 'Warships' in the early 1970s. Standing at Yeovil Junction with a down service on 25 October 1977 is No 33 013. The locomotive carries the Southern Region route headcode 62; these two-character headcodes remained in use long after the BR four-character codes ceased to be displayed. The 33s would remain in charge of Waterloo–Exeter services until 1980, with standard consists of eight Mk 1 coaches in winter and nine in summer. *Paul Shannon*

Motorail services in the 1970s and 1980s included trains for holidaymakers to and from Newton Abbot and St Austell. No 50 007 *Hercules* approaches Castle Cary station on 28 August 1982 with the 07.30 departure from Paddington — a cars-only working, passengers travelling on a separate train. The use of open wagons on Motorail trains ceased in the late 1980s, but a scaled-down service using specially adapted vans operated between London and Penzance until 2005. *Michael Mensing*

After the mass cull of station goods yards in the 1960s, those facilities that survived tended to concentrate on specific traffic flows, often delivered by the trainload. Bridgwater goods yard remained open for UKF fertiliser from Ince & Elton as well as for nuclear flasks to Hinkley Point power station and for general goods, including packaged drinks. No 47 330 shunts PWA fertiliser vans at Bridgwater on 28 July 1987 before departing with train 6M34, the 17.40 Tuesdays-only service to Ince & Elton. *Paul Shannon*

With its headcode display intact but now set to '0O00' in line with BR policy, Class 45 'Peak' No 45 060 *Sherwood Forester* is about to leave Exeter St Davids with the 10.23 Manchester–Plymouth service on 29 September 1976. Although no Class 45s were allocated to the Western Region at that time, the class made frequent appearances on cross-country trains to and from Devon and Cornwall. *Hugh Ballantyne*

45 058 skirts the famous sea wall at Langstone Rock, between Dawlish and Dawlish Warren, with the 10.35 from Paignton to Leeds on 18 August 1979. Formerly No D97, this locomotive was a long-standing Toton machine, although its duties took it regularly to Western and Eastern Region territory as well as up and down the Midland main line. *Hugh Ballantyne*

Class 52 'Western' No D1008 *Western Harrier* has just emerged from Parson's Tunnel, on the approach to Teignmouth, with a down passenger service on 31 August 1972. By that time very few 'Warships' and 'Hymeks' remained in service, and soon the 'Westerns' would be the last relics of the ill-fated diesel-hydraulic policy pursued by the Western Region. *Gavin Morrison*

A busy scene at Paignton on 29 August 1981 as No 50 006 *Neptune* departs with an up express under the gaze of dozens of holidaymakers. An unidentified 'Peak' stands on the adjacent track. *Neptune* was one of the first two Class 50s to undergo refurbishment at Doncaster, finally emerging in September 1979 after two years out of service. The second of the class to be withdrawn, it was condemned in July 1987 and despatched to Vic Berry's scrapyard in Leicester. *John Edgington*

The Western Region received a small allocation of Class 46 'Peaks' in the late 1960s, and in the 1970s further examples were drafted in to replace withdrawn diesel-hydraulics. No 46 018 arrives at Totnes with a down train on 27 September 1979. Although on average slightly younger than the Class 45s, the Class 46s succumbed to the axe first; No 46 018 was withdrawn in December 1983, and the class was extinct on the main line by 1984. *Paul Shannon*

Class 37s started appearing on Cornish china-clay trains in 1978 and gradually strengthened their foothold as other classes moved away. No 37 299 prepares to depart from Bodmin General station with empty UCV 'clay hoods' for Wenford Bridge on 3 August 1982. This was a tortuous operation by today's standards: the wagons were conveyed first from Fowey to Bodmin General, including a reversal at Bodmin Road, then in two portions from Bodmin General to Boscarne Junction, and finally by a Class 08 shunter from Boscarne Junction to Wenford Bridge. No 37 299 moved away from Cornwall in late 1982; it was later renumbered 37 426 upon refurbishment and conversion to an ETH machine and remained in use until 2003. *Paul Shannon*

Above:
The former Great Western Railway goods shed at Lostwithiel provides a frame for No 50 047 *Swiftsure* **as it calls on 3 August 1982 with a Plymouth–Penzance stopping train — a comparatively light duty for this express-passenger type. No 50 047 survived until April 1988; by then it was due for an overhaul, and its withdrawal yielded a useful supply of spares for the survivors.** *Paul Shannon*

Below:
A blue Class 47 with blue-and-grey coaching stock epitomises the era of the BR corporate image, disdained by many enthusiasts who fondly remembered the 'Warships' and 'Westerns' of the 1960s and early 1970s. No 47 475 rounds the curve into Par station with the 09.30 from Liverpool Lime Street to Penzance on 3 August 1982. The locomotive was delivered new to the Western Region as No D1603 in 1964 but was based at Bescot by the time of the photograph. *Paul Shannon*

Above:

The repainting of Class 08 shunters was a low priority, and many examples retained BR blue throughout the 1980s. On the morning of 16 February 1988 one of the St Blazey pilots, No 08 955, approaches St Blazey Yard with a trip working from Pontsmill comprising two PRA wagons with china clay for Corpach paper mill. *Paul Shannon*

Below:

China clay was the staple traffic on Speedlink services to and from Cornwall, being transported in bulk, slurry and bagged forms and used a wide variety of wagon types. On 29 July 1983 No 46 028 prepares to set back out of St Blazey Yard with train 6C43, the 15.20 departure to Severn Tunnel Junction. The load comprises two ferry vans for Basel, a PBA hopper from Drinnick Mill to Cliffe Vale, a VDA van from St Blazey to Mossend and five PRA wagons from Pontsmill to Corpach. *Paul Shannon*